# MORE

# SONGS & BALLADS OF IRELAND

### A SECOND COLLECTION OF 40 IRISH SONGS
WITH COMPLETE WORDS, MUSIC AND GUITAR CHORDS

OSSIAN

Special thanks to Tom Munnelly for the use of
"In Scartaglen there lived a Lass', as collected
by  him in Kerry

Every effort has been made to ascertain the rights
on each song. The publishers beg to be informed of
any unintended infringements on any still existing rights.
Apart from the indicated copyright songs, all other
songs in this collection are copyright arrangements
by John Loesberg.
The editor thankfully acknowledges permission
given by publishers and composers of copyright material.

Printed at Watermans Printers, Cork, for
**OSSIAN PUBLICATIONS,**
**PO BOX 84,**
**CORK, IRELAND**

ISBN 0 946005 54 0
OMB 77

# Contents

# The Wild Rover

I've been a wild ro-ver for ma-ny's the year,_____ And I've
spent all me mo-ney on whis-key and beer,_____ And now I'm re-
tur-ning with gold in great store,_____ And I ne-ver will play the wild
ro-ver no more, And it's No, Nay, Ne-ver,_____
_____ No Nay Ne-ver No more,_____ Will I play_____
_____ the wild ro-ver,_____ No, Ne-ver_____ No more.

I went to an alehouse I used to frequent,
And I told the landlady my money was spent.
I asked her for credit she answered me 'Nay,
Such custom as yours I could have every day.'
CHORUS

I brought up from my pockets ten sovereigns bright
And the landlady's eyes opened wide with delight.
She said 'I have whiskeys and wines of the best,
And the words that I told you were only in jest.'
CHORUS

I'll go home to my parents, confess what I've done,
And I'll ask them to pardon their prodigal son.
And when they've caressed me as oft times before,
I never will play the wild rover no more.
CHORUS

OMB 77

# The Mountains of Mourne

Percy French

Oh, Ma - ry this Lon - don's a won - der - ful sight with the
peo - ple here wor - king by day and by night, They don't sow po - ta - toes nor
bar - ley nor wheat, But there's gangs of them dig - ging for
gold in the street, At least when I asked them that's what I was told, So I
just took a hand at this dig - ging for gold, But for all that I found there I
might as well be, Where the moun - tains of Mourne sweep down to the sea.

I believe that when writing a wish you expressed
As to how the fine ladies of London were dressed.
Well if you believe me, when asked to a ball,
They don't wear a top to their dresses at all.
Oh, I've seen them myself, and you couldn't in truth
Say if they were bound for a ball or a bath.
Don't be starting them fashions now Mary Macree
Where the mountains of Mourne sweep down to the sea.

I've seen England's king from the top of a bus -
I never knew him, though he means to know us;
And though by the Saxon we once were oppressed,
Still I cheered - God forgive me - I cheered with the rest.
And now that he's visited Erin's green shore,
We'll be much better friends than we've been heretofore.
When we've got all we want we're as quiet as can be,
Where the mountains of Mourne sweep down to the sea.

You remember young Peter O'Loughlin of course -
Well now he is here at the head of the force.
I met him today, I was crossing the Strand,
And he stopped the whole street with one wave of his hand.
And there we stood talking of days that are gone,
While the whole population of London looked on;
But for all these great powers he's wishful, like me,
To be back where dark Mourne sweeps down to the sea.

There's beautiful girls here - oh, never you mind
With beautiful shapes Nature never designed.
And lovely complexions, all roses and cream (crame)
But O'Loughlin remarked with regard to the same,
That if at those roses you venture to sip,
The colours might all come away on your lip;
So I'll wait for the wild rose that's waiting for me,
Where the mountains of Mourne sweep down to the sea.

*Newry River.*

7

# The Rose of Tralee

By E.M. Spencer

The pale moon was ri-sing a-bove the green moun-tains, The sun was de-

cli-ning be-neath the blue sea, When I stray'd with my love to the

pure crys-tal foun-tain, That stands in the beau-ti-ful vale of Tra-

lee. She was love-ly and fair as the rose of the sum-mer, Yet

'twas not her beau-ty a-lone that won me, Oh, no 'twas the truth in her

eye e-ver daw-ning, That made me love Ma-ry, the Rose of Tra-lee.

The cool shades of evening their mantles were spreading,
And Mary, all smiles, sat listening to me,
The moon thro' the valley, her pale rays were shedding,
When I won the heart of the Rose of Tralee.
Tho' lovely and fair as the rose of the summer,
Yet 'twas not her beauty alone that won me,
Oh no, 'twas truth in her eye ever dawning,
That made me love Mary, the Rose of Tralee.

# The Foggy Dew

As down the glen one Eas-ter morn to a ci-ty fair rode I, There
ar-med lines of mar-ching men in squad-rons passed me by. No
pipe did hum, no bat-tle drum did sound its dread tat-too, But the
An-ge-lus bell o'er the Lif-fey swell, rang out through the fog-gy dew.

'Twas England bade our Wild Geese 'Go', that small nations might be free
But their lonely graves are by Suvla's waves or the fringe of the great North Sea.
Oh, had they died by Pearse's side, or fought with Cathal Brugha,
Their names we'd keep where the Fenians sleep, 'neath the shroud of the Foggy Dew.

Right proudly high over Dublin town they hung out the flag of war.
'Twas better to die 'neath an Irish sky than at Suvla or Sud el Bar;
And from the plains of Royal Meath strong men came hurrying through,
While Brittania's Huns, with their great big guns, sailed in through the Foggy Dew.

But the bravest fell and the requiem bell rang mournfully and clear,
For those who died that Easter tide, in the springtime of the year;
While the world did gaze with deep amaze, at those fearless men but few,
Who bore the fight, that freedom's light might shine through the Foggy Dew.

OMB 77

# The Rose of Allendale

The morn was fair, the skies were clear, no breath came o'er the sea, When Mary left her high-land home and wan-dered forth with me, Though flo-wers deck'd the moun-tain-side and fra-grance fill'd the vale, By far the sweet-est flo-wer there was the rose of Al-len-dale,

*Chorus*

Was the rose of Al-len-dale, Was the rose of Al-len-dale, By far the sweet-est flo-wer there was the rose of Al-len-dale.

Where'er I wandered, east or west,
Tho' fate began to lour,
A solace still she was to me,
In sorrow's lonely hour.
When tempests lashed our lonely barque,
And rent her shiv'ring sail,
One maiden form withstood the storm,
'Twas the Rose of Allendale.

And when my fever'd lips were parched
On Afric's burning sands,
She whispered hopes of happiness
And tales of distant lands.
My life has been a wilderness
Unblest by fortune's gale;
Had fate not linked my lot to hers,
The Rose of Allendale.

THE HORIZONTAL FORMATION, GIANT'S CAUSEWAY.

11

# Slievenamon

By C.J. Kickham

A - lone, all a - lone,___ by the wave - wash'd___ strand___ all a -
lone in a crow - ded___ hall._____ The hall it is gay___ and the
waves they are grand___ but my heart is not here at___ all._____
___ It flies far - a - way,___ by night___and by day,___ to the time and the
joys that are gone,_____ And I ne - ver can for - get___ the sweet
mai - den I met,___ In the val - ley near Slieve - na - mon._____

It was not the grace of her queenly air,
Nor her cheek of the rose's glow,
Nor her soft black eyes, nor her flowing hair,
Nor was it her lily-white brow.
'Twas the soul of truth and of melting ruth,
And the smile of summer's dawn,
That stole my heart away, one mild summer day,
In the valley near Slievenamon.

In the festive hall, by the star-watched shore,
My restless spirit cries:
'My love, oh my love, shall I ne'er see you more.
And my land will you e'er uprise.
By night and by day I ever, ever pray,
While lonely my life flows on.
To our flag unrolled and my true love to enfold,
In the valley near Slievenamon.

# I'll Tell My Ma

I'll tell me ma, when I go home, the boys won't leave the girls a-lone. They

pull my hair, they stole my comb, and that's all-right till I go home.

She is hand-some, she is pret-ty, she's the belle of Bel-fast ci-ty,

she is cour-tin', one, two, three, Please won't you tell me who is she?

Albert Mooney says he loves her,
All the boys are fighting for her,
They rap at the door and they ring at the bell,
Saying 'Oh my true-love are you well?'
Out she comes as white as snow,
Rings on her fingers, bells on her toes,
Old Jenny Murphy says she'll die,
If she doesn't get the fellow with the roving eye.

Let the wind and the rain and the hail blow high
And the snow come shovelling from the sky
She's as nice as apple pie
And she'll get her own lad by and by.
When she gets a lad of her own
She won't tell her ma when she gets home
Let them all come as they will,
But its Albert Mooney she loves still.

OMB 77

# Bold Thady Quill

By J.T. Gleeson

Ye maids of Du - hal - low who're anx - ious for cour - tin' a word of ad - vice I will give un - to ye: Pro - ceed to Ban - teer, to the ath - le - tic spor - tin' and hand in ye'r names to the club com - mit - tee, But do not com - mence a - ny sketch of your pro - gress 'till a car - riage you see co - min' o - ver the hill, And down thro' the val - leys and hills of Kil - cor - ney with that Mus - ker - ry sports - man the bould Tha - dy Quill. For ram - blin' for ro - vin' for foot - ball or cour - tin' for emp - tin' a bowl sure as fast as you'd fill In all your days ro - vin' you'd find none so jo - vial as the Mus - ker - ry sports - man the bold Tha - dy Quill.

Thady was famous in many other places;
At the athletic meeting held out in Cloghroe
He won the long jump without throwing off his braces
Goin' fifty-four feet every sweep he would throw.
At the puttin' of the weight there was a Dublin man foremost,
But Thady outreached and exceeded him still.
And around the whole field rang the wild ringing chorus
'Here's luck to our hero, the bold Thady Quill'.
Muskerry sportsman the bould Thady Quill.

At the great hurlin' match between Cork and Tipperary
('Twas played in the park by the banks of the Lee)
Our own darlin' boys were afraid of being baten
So they send for bold Thady to Ballinagree.
He hurled the ball left and right in their faces,
And show'd those Tipp'rary boys learning and skill
If they came in this way, shure he surely would brain 'em
And the papers were full of praise for old Thade Quill.

In the year ninety-one before Parnell was taken,
Thade was outrageously breaking the peace.
He got a light sentence for causing commotion,
And six months hard labour for batin' police.
But in spite of coercion he's still agitatin'
Ev'ry drop of his life's blood he's willing to spill,
To gain for old Ireland complete liberation,
'Till then there's no rest for me', says bold Thady Quill.

At the Cork Exhibition there was a fair lady,
Whose fortune exceeded a million or more:
But a bad constitution had ruined her completely,
And medical treatment had failed o'er and o'er.
'Oh Mama', said she 'I know what'll cure me
And all me diseases most certainly kill,
Give over your doctors and medical treatment
I'd rather one shake outa bold Thady Quill!'

OMB 77

# The Irish Rover

In the year of our Lord, eight-een hun-dred and six, We set
sail from the Coal Quay of Cork, We were sail-ing a-way with a
car-go of bricks, For the grand ci-ty hall in New York. We'd an
el-e-gant craft, it was rigged fore and aft, And how the trade winds
drove_____ her; She had twen-ty-three masts and she
stood sev'-ral blasts, And they called her the I-rish Ro-ver.

There was Barney Magee from the banks of the Lee;
There was Hogan from County Tyrone.
There was Johnny McGurk, who was scared stiff of work,
And a chap from Westmeath named Malone.
There was Slugger O'Toole, who was drunk as a rule,
And fighting Bill Tracy from Dover;
And your man Mick McCann from the banks of the Bann,
Was the skipper on the Irish Rover.

# Nora

By Sean O'Casey

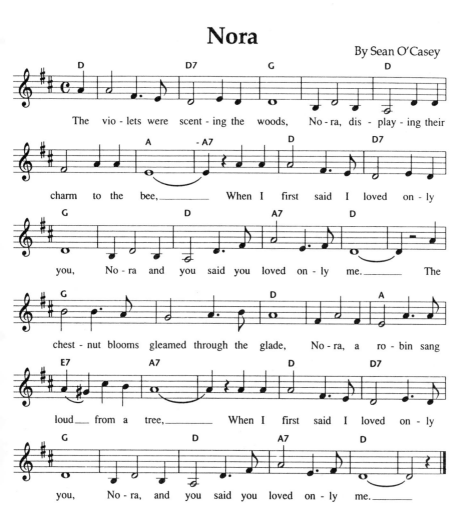

The chestnut blooms gleamed through the glade, Nora,
A robin sang loud from a tree,
When I first said I loved only you, Nora,
And you said you loved only me.

The golden-robed daffodils shone, Nora,
And danced in the breeze on the lea,
When I first said I loved only you, Nora,
And you said you loved only me.

The trees, birds and bees sang a song, Nora,
Of happier transports to be,
When I first said I loved only you, Nora,
And you said you loved only me.

OMB 77

# I Know My Love

I know my love by her way of walk - ing and I know my
love by her way of talk - ing and I know my love by her
suit of blue but if my love leaves me_____ what will I do?____

*Chorus*
And yet she cries 'I love him the best.' But a troub - led mind
sure can know no rest,___ And yet she cries___ 'Bon - ny boys are few,'
— Yet if my love leaves me,___ what will I do?_____

There is a dance house in Mardyke,
And 'tis there my dear love goes every night:
And he takes a strange girl all on his knee,
And don't you think but it troubles me.

If my love knew I could wash and wring,
And if my love knew I could weave and spin,
I could make a suit all of the finest kind,
But the want of money, it leaves me behind.

# On the Banks of the Roses

On the banks of the Ro - ses, my love and I sat down and
I took out my vio - lin to play my love a tune, In the
mid - dle of the tune, oh, she sighed and she said: 'O - ro
John - ny, love - ly John - ny, would you leave me.

Oh when I was a young man I heard my father say,
That he'd rather see me dead and buried in the clay,
Sooner than be married to any runaway,
By the lovely sweet Banks of the Roses.

Oh then I am no runaway and soon I'll let them know,
I can take a good glass or can leave it alone;
And the man that doesn't like me, he can keep his daughter at home,
And young Johnny will go roving with another.

And if ever I get married 'twill be in the month of May,
When the leaves they are green and the meadows they are gay,
And I and my true love can sit and sport and play,
On the lovely sweet Banks of the Roses.

19

# Sally Gardens

By W.B. Yeats

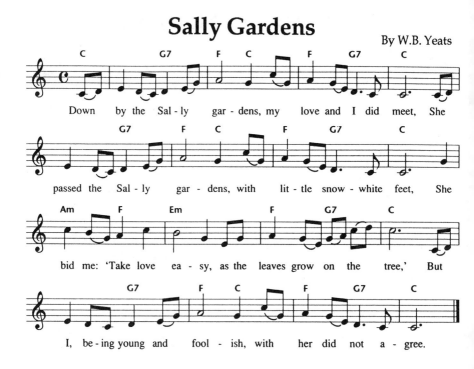

Down by the Sal - ly gar - dens, my love and I did meet, She

passed the Sal - ly gar - dens, with lit - tle snow - white feet, She

bid me: 'Take love ea - sy, as the leaves grow on the tree,' But

I, be - ing young and fool - ish, with her did not a - gree.

In a field down by the river, my love and I did stand
And on my leaning shoulder, she laid her snow-white hand.
She bid me take life easy, as the grass grows on the weirs;
But I was young and foolish and now am full of tears.

Down by the Sally gardens, my love and I did meet,
She passed the Sally gardens, with little snow-white feet.
She bid me take love easy, as the leaves grow on the tree;
But I, being young and foolish, with her did not agree.

# The West's Awake

When all be-side a vi-gil keep, the west's a-sleep, the west's a-sleep, A - las, and well may E - rin weep, that Con - naught lies in slum - ber deep, There lake and plain smile fair and free, 'mid rocks their guard - ian chi - val - ry, Sing: Oh, let man learn li - ber - ty, from crash - ing wind and lash - ing sea.

That chainless wave and lovely land,
Freedom and Nationhood demand.
Be sure the great God never planned
For slumb'ring slaves a home so grand.
And long a proud and haughty race
Honour'd and sentinell'd the place.
Sing: Oh not e'en their sons' disgrace
Can quite destroy their glory's trace.

For often in O'Connor's van,
To triumph dashed each Connaught clan
And fleet as deer the Normans ran
Through Curlew's Pass and Ardrahan;
And later times saw deeds as brave,
And glory guards Clanricarde's grave;
Sing: Oh they died their land to save
At Aughrim's slopes and Shannon's wave.

And if, when all a vigil keep,
The west's asleep, the west's asleep
Alas and well may Erin weep
That Connaught lies in slumber deep.
But hark, a voice like thunder spake,
The west's awake, the west's awake.
Sing: Oh hurrah, let England quake
We'll watch till death for Erin's sake.

OMB 77

# The Green Fields of America

Our ship is__ now__ wait - ing, her an - chor__ she's__
weigh - ing. Fare-__ well to the__ land____ that I'm goin' to
leave. My__ Bet - sy has__ part-__ ed with__ fa - ther and__
mo - ther. With__ me for to cross o'er the wide west - ern wave.

So hasten dear Betsy, my dear blue-eyed lassie,
Bid farewell to your mother and come along with me;
I'll do my endeavour to make your heart cheery,
Till we reach the green fields of Americay.

There's brandy in Quebec at just tenpence a quart boys,
There's gin in New Brunswick at a penny a glass,
There's rum in the town that they call Montreal,
And we will drink hearty each one as we pass.

So cheer up your hearts all you lads and young lasses,
There's gold here among us and lots of it too;
Success to the hearts that have courage to venture,
Misfortune to him or to her that would rue.

Farewell to the groves of the sweet County Wicklow,
Likewise to the girls of old Erin around;
May their hearts be as merry as ever I wish them,
Although far away on the ocean I'm bound.

And if ever it happens in some foreign climate,
That a poor friendless Irishman should come in my way,
With the best I can give him I'll make him right welcome,
In my own habitation in Americay.

*Cascade in the Dargle.*

23

# Lough Sheelin's Side

Farewell my country, a long farewell, My bitter anguish no tongue can tell. For I must fly o'er the ocean wide, From the home I loved by Lough Shee-lin Side.

Fond mem'ries come 'till my heart grows sad,
And vengeful thoughts 'till my brain goes mad;
When I think of Eileen my fair young bride,
In the churchyard lone, by Lough Sheelin's side.

When I first wooed her, so fair and young,
With her artless airs and her guileless tongue;
All other maidens she far outvied,
On the lonely banks of Lough Sheelin's side.

So proud was I of my girl so tall,
And envied most by the young men all;
When I brought her blushing with bashful pride,
To my cottage home by Lough Sheelin's side.

But ah! our joys were too full to last;
The landlord came our bright hopes to blast,
In vain we pleaded for mercy - no!
But he hurled us forth in the blinding snow.

Not one dare open for us their door
Or else his vengeance would reach them sure;
My Eileen faint in my arms died
As the snow lay deep on the mountain side.

I raised my hand to the heavens above,
And I said one prayer for my lifeless love;
May the God of justice, I wildly cried,
Avenge the death of my murdered bride.

We laid her down in the churchyard low,
Where in the springtime sweet daisies grow;
I shed no tears for the fount has dried,
On that woeful night by Lough Sheelin's side.

Farewell, my country, farewell for e'er,
The big ship's waiting I must prepare.
But my fond heart it shall still abide,
In my Eileen's grave by Lough Sheelin's side.

ENTRANCE TO NEW GRANGE.

OMB 77

# The Old Triangle

By B. Behan

A— hung - ry feel - ing, came o'er me steal___
ing. And the mice were squeal - ing. In my pri - son cell.___
___ And that old tri - an - gle went jin - gle, jan___
gle, All a - long the__ banks of the Ro - yal Ca - nal___

To begin the morning, the warden's bawling:
'Get out of bed and clean up your cell'.
And that old triangle went jingle, jangle
Along the banks of the Royal Canal.

On a fine spring evening, the lag lay dreaming,
The seagulls wheeling high above the wall,
And the old triangle went jingle, jangle
Along the banks of the Royal Canal.

The screw was peeping, the lag was sleeping,
While he lay weeping for his girl Sal,
And the old triangle went jingle, jangle
Along the banks of the Royal Canal.

The wind was rising and the day declining,
As I lay pining in my prison cell,
And the old triangle went jingle, jangle
Along the banks of the Royal Canal.

In the female prison there are seventy women,
I wish it was with them that I did dwell,
Then that old triangle could jingle jangle
Along the banks of the Royal Canal.

The day was dying and the wind was sighing,
As I lay crying in my prison cell,
And the old triangle went jingle, jangle
Along the banks of the Royal Canal.

# Since Maggie Went Away

By Sean O'Casey

No more I stroll, no more I stroll, a - long the bo - reen, I
see the scar - let pop - pies play a - mid the corn green, No
more be - neath the hedge I watch the but - ter - flies at play, For my
heart is filled with woe with woe, since Mag - gie went a - way.

The sweet wild rose, the sweet wild rose,
That lov'd to see us there,
And seem'd to bid us hope, now droops,
And tells me to despair;
The linnet sings his song unheard,
Perched on a leafy spray -
Ah, my heart is filled with woe, with woe,
Since Maggie went away.

The gentle flowers, the gentle flowers,
Their happy charm is fled,
And now they seem like blossoms strewn,
Above the silent dead.
They're symbols now of sorrow deep,
And life's swift, sure decay -
Ah, my heart is filled with woe, with woe,
Since Maggie went away.

The heartless sun, the heatless sun,
With splendour gilds the skies,
And mocks with smiling beams a heart
That now can only sigh;
Shine on, bright sun, shine on, while I
Could curse thy proud display,
For my heart is filled with woe, with woe,
Since Maggie went away.

Then welcome grief, then welcome grief,
Man's warm, true-hearted friend,
For tho' all things be false, thou still art,
Faithful to the end;
And now I walk alone with thee,
Till life turns into clay -
For my heart is filled with woe, with woe,
Since Maggie went away.

OMB 77

# Raglan Road

By P. Kavanagh

On Rag - lan Road of an Au - tumn day, I saw her first and knew, that her dark hair would weave a snare that I might one day rue, I saw the dan - ger and I passed, a - long the en - chant - ed way, And I said let grief be a fal - len leaf at the dawn - ing of the day.

On Grafton Street in November we tripped lightly along the ledge
Of a deep ravine where can be seen the worth of passion play,
The Queen of Hearts still making tarts and I not making hay,
Oh, I loved too much and by such and such
Is happiness thrown away.

I gave her gifts of the mind, I gave her secret signs
That's known to the artists who have known the true gods of sound and stone,
And her words and tint without stint, I gave her poems to say,
With her own name there and her own dark hair
Like clouds over fields of May.

On a quiet street where old ghosts meet, I see her walking now,
Away from me so hurriedly, my reason must allow,
That I had loved not as I should, a creature made of clay,
When the angel woos the clay he'll lose
His wings at the dawn of day.

# Slieve Gallen Braes

As I went out one morn-ing all in the month of May. To view all your moun-tains and val-leys so gay. I was think-ing of the flow-ers all a-go-ing to de-cay. That bloom a-round yon bon-ny, bon-ny, Slieve Gal-len Braes.

How oft in the morning with my dog and my gun
I roam through the glens for joy and for fun
But those days are now all over and I must go away,
So farewell unto ye, bonny, bonny, Slieve Gallen Braes.

How oft of an evening and the sun in the west
I roved hand in hand with the one I loved best.
But the hopes of youth are vanished and now I'm far away,
So farewell unto ye, bonny, bonny, Slieve Gallen Braes.

Oh! it was not the want of employment at home
That caused us poor exiles in sorrow to roam,
But those tyrannising landlords, they would not let us stay,
So farewell unto ye, bonny, bonny, Slieve Gallen Braes.

OMB 77

# The Galway Shawl

In O - ran - more, in the Coun - ty Gal - way one plea - sant ev - en - ing in the month of May, I spied a dam - sel she was young and hand - some her beau - ty fair - ly took my breath a - way.

She wore no jewels or costly diamonds
No paint or powder, no none at all.
She wore a bonnet with a ribbon on it
And around her shoulder was the Galway shawl.

As we kept on walking, she kept on talking
'Til her father's cottage came into view.
Said she 'Come in,Sir, and meet my father
And for to please him play the "Foggy Dew."'

I played the 'Blackbird' and the 'Stack of Barley'
'Rodney's Glory' and the 'Foggy Dew'
She sang each note like an Irish Linnet
And the tears flowed in her eyes of blue.

'Twas early, early, all in the morning
I hit the road for old Donegal.
Said she 'Goodbye Sir' as she cried
And me heart remained with the Galway shawl.

LEATHER OUTER CASE OF THE BOOK OF ARMAGH, SHOWING THE EARLY
IRISH TRACERY ORNAMENTATION.

# The Golden Jubilee

Way down in the Coun - ty Ker - ry. In the place they call Tra -
lee, A fine old coup - le they lived there, called Kate and Pat Mc - Gee: They were
goin' to hold a par - ty on their Gold - en Ju - bi - lee, And
Kate said she to Pat Mc - Gee "Come lis - ten here to me:"

*Chorus:*

"Put on your oul' knee breech - es, And your coat of em' - rald green. Take
off that hat, me dar - lin' Pat, put on your oul' Cau - been. For to -
day's our Gold - en Wed - ding, And we want them all to know, The
way we looked when we were wed, just fif - ty years a - go."

Ah, well do I remember when we danced on the village green,
You held me in your arms, dear Pat, and called me your colleen.
Your hair was like the raven's wing, but now 'tis turning grey,
Come over here, oul' sweetheart dear, and hear what I've to say.

Ah, well do I remember when first I was your bride,
In the little chapel yonder there, where we sat side by side.
Of good things we've had many, of troubles we've had few:
Come over here, oul' sweetheart dear, and here's what you must do.

Mount Brendan

OMB 77

# The Next Market Day

A maid went to Comb-er her mar-kets to learn, To
sell for her mam-my three hanks of fine yarn, She
met a young man on the King's own high-way, Which
caused this young dam-sel to dal-ly and stray.

*Chorus:* Come sit down be-side me I mean you no harm, Come
sit down be-side me this new tune to learn, Here
are three new guin-eas, your mam-my to pay, So
leave off your lear-nin' till next mar-ket day.

She sat down beside him , the grass was so green,
The day was the fairest that ever was seen.
The look in your eye beats a morning in May,
I could sit by your side till the next market day

Now as she went homeward, the words he had said,
And the tune that he sung her still ring in her head,
I'll search for that lad be it land or by sea,
Till he learns me the tune to 'The Next Market Day.'

# The Lambs on the Green Hills

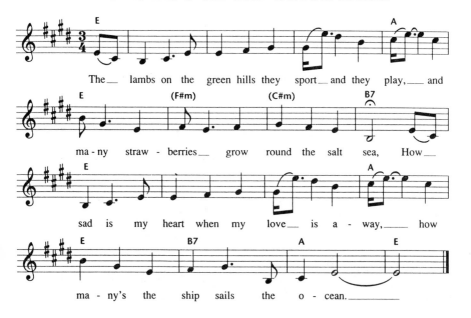

The_ lambs on the green hills they sport_ and they play,_ and
ma - ny straw - berries_ grow round the salt sea, How_
sad is my heart when my love_ is a - way,_ how
ma - ny's the ship sails the o - cean._

The bride and bride's party to church they did go,
The bride she rode foremost, she bears the best show,
But I followed after with my heart full of woe,
To see my love wed to another.

The first place I saw her was in the church stand,
Gold rings on her finger and her love by the hand.
Says I, 'My wee lassie, I will be the man,
Although you are wed to another.'

The next place I saw her was on the way home.
I ran on before her, not knowing where to roam,
Says I, 'My wee lassie, I'll be by your side,
Although you are wed to another.'

'Stop, stop', says the groomsman, 'Till I speak a word,
Will you venture your life on the point of my sword?
For courting so slowly you've lost this fair maid,
So, begone, for you'll never enjoy her.'

Oh, make now my grave both large, wide and deep,
And sprinkle it over with flowers so sweet,
And lay me down in it to take my last sleep,
For that's the best way to forget her.

OMB 77

# Kevin Barry

In Mount-joy jail, one mon-day mor-ning, High up - on the gal-lows tree, Ke-vin Bar - ry gave his young life, For the cause of lib-er-ty, But a lad of eight-een sum-mers, Yet___ no one can de-ny, As he walked to death that mor-ning, He proud-ly held his head on high.

Just before he faced the hangmen, in his dreary prison cell,
British soldiers tortured Barry, just because he would not tell,
The names of his brave companions and other things they wished to know,
'Turn informer, or we'll kill you.' Kevin Barry answered 'No'.

Calmly standing to attention, while he bade his last farewell,
To his broken-hearted mother, whose grief no one can tell.
For the cause he proudly cherished, this sad parting had to be,
Then to death walked softly smiling, that old Ireland might be free.

Another martyr for old Ireland, another murder for the crown,
Whose brutal laws may kill the Irish, but can't keep their spirits down.
Lads like Barry are no cowards, from the foe they will not fly,
Lads like Barry will free Ireland, for her sake they'll live and die.

# Come to the Hills

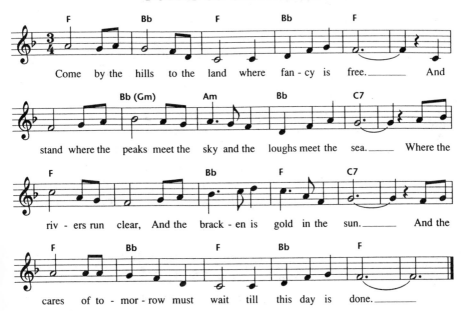

Come by the hills to the land where fan-cy is free.____ And stand where the peaks meet the sky and the loughs meet the sea.____ Where the riv-ers run clear, And the brack-en is gold in the sun.____ And the cares of to-mor-row must wait till this day is done.____

Come to the hills where life is a song
And sing where the birds fill the air
With their joy all day long.
Where the trees sway in time
And even the wind sings in tune
And the cares of tomorrow can wait
Till this day is done.

Come by the hills to the land
Where legend remains,
Where stories of old filled the heart
And they yet come again;
Where our past has been lost
And our future has still to be won
And the cares of tomorrow must wait
Till this day is done.

*Repeat first verse.*

OMB 77

# Spinningwheel Song

By John F. Waller

Mel-low the moon-light to shine is be-gin-ning, __ close by the win-dow young Ei-leen is spin-ning, __ Bent o'er the fire her blind grand-moth-er sit-ting, __ Croon-ing and moan-ing and drow-si-ly knit-ting.

*Chorus*

Mer-ri-ly, cheer-i-ly, noise-less-ly whir-ring __ Spins the wheel, rings the wheel while the foot's stir-ring __ Light-ly and bright-ly and air-i-ly ring-ing, __ Sounds the sweet voice of the young mai-den sing-ing. __

What's the noise that I hear at the window I wonder,
''Tis the little birds chirping the holly-bush under'
'What makes you be shoving and moving your stool on,
An' singing, all wrong, that old song of "The Coolun"?'

There's a form at the casement - the form of her true love,
And he whispers, with face bent: 'I'm waiting for you, love,
Get up from the stool, through the lattice step lightly,
We'll rove in the grove while the moon's shining brightly.'

CHORUS:
Merrily, cheerily, noiselessly whirring,
Spins the wheel, rings the wheel, while the foot's stirring.
Sprightly and lightly and airily ringing,
Trills the sweet voice of the young maiden singing.

The maid shakes her head, on her lip lays her fingers,
Steals up from the stool - longs to go and yet lingers.
A frightened glance turns to her drowsy grandmother,
Puts one foot on the stool, spins the wheel with the other.

CHORUS:
Lazily, easily, swings now the wheel round,
Slowly and lowly is heard now the reel's sound,
Noiseless and light to the lattice above her,
The maid steps - then leaps to the arms of her lover.

CHORUS:
Slower - and slower - and slower the wheel swings
Lower - and lower - and lower the reel rings;
Ere the reel and the wheel stop their ringing and moving,
Through the grove the young lovers by moonlight are roving.

ARDMORE, COUNTY WATERFORD.

OMB 77

# Johnny, I Hardly Knew Yeh

While going the road to sweet A - thy, ha - roo,— ha - roo,— While
going the road to sweet A - thy, ha - roo,———— ha -
roo,———— While going the road to sweet A - thy, a
stick in my hand and a tear in my eye, A dole - ful dam - sel
I heard cry: 'John - ny I hard - ly knew yeh.

Chorus (*to the same tune as verse above*):
With drums and guns and guns and drums, ha-roo, ha-roo,
With drums and guns and guns and drums, ha-roo, ha-roo,
With drums and guns and guns and drums the enemy nearly slew yeh,
My darling dear you look so queer, Johnny I hardly knew yeh.

Where are the eyes that looked so mild, ha-roo, ha-roo,
Where are the eyes that looked so mild, ha-roo, ha-roo,
Where are the eyes that looked so mild,
When my poor heart you first beguiled,
Why did you skedaddle from me and the child,
Johnny I hardly knew yeh.

Where are the legs with which you run, ha-roo, ha-roo
Where are the legs with which you run, ha-roo, ha-roo
Where are the legs with which you run,
When you went to shoulder a gun,
Indeed your dancing days are done,
Johnny I hardly knew yeh.

It grieved my heart to see you sail, ha-roo, ha-roo
It grieved my heart to see you sail, ha-roo, ha-roo
It grieved my heart to see you sail
Though from my heart you took leg-bail,
Like a cod you're doubled up head and tail,
Johnny I hardly knew yeh.

You haven't an arm and you haven't a leg, ha-roo, ha-roo
You haven't an arm and you haven't a leg, ha-roo, ha-roo
You haven't an arm and you haven't a leg,
You're an eyeless, noseless, chickenless egg,
You'll have to be put in a bowl to beg,
Johnny I hardly knew yeh.

I'm happy for to see you home, ha-roo, ha-roo
I'm happy for to see you home, ha-roo, ha-roo
I'm happy for to see you home,
All from the island of Sulloon,
So low in the flesh so high in the bone,
Johnny I hardly knew yeh.

But sad as it is to see you so, ha-roo, har-oo
But sad as it is to see you so, ha-roo, har-oo
But sad as it is to see you so,
And to think of you now as an object of woe,
Your Peggy'll still keep you on as her beau,
Johnny I hardly knew yeh.

ANTRIM CASTLE.

41

# I Never Will Marry

I ne-ver will mar - ry,_____ I'll be no man's wife,_____
_____ I in-tend to stay sing - le,_____ for the rest of my life._____

One day as I rambled down by the sea shore,
The wind it did whistle and the waters did roar.

I heard a poor maiden make a pitiful cry,
She sounded so lonesome at the waters nearby.

I never will marry, I'll be no man's wife,
I intend to stay single, for the rest of my life.

The shells in the ocean will be my deathbed,
And the fish in the water swim over my head.

My love's gone and left me, he's the one I adore,
I never will see him, no never, no more.

She plunged her fair body in the water so deep,
She closed her pretty blue eyes in the water to sleep.

I never will marry, I'll be no man's wife,
I intend to stay single, for the rest of my life.

# A Bunch of Thyme

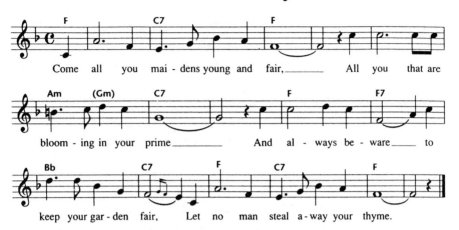

Come all you mai - dens young and fair,_____ All you that are
bloom - ing in your prime_____ And al - ways be - ware_____ to
keep your gar - den fair, Let no man steal a - way your thyme.

For thyme it is a precious thing
And thyme brings all things to my mind
Thyme with all its flavours, along with all its joys,
Thyme brings all things to my mind.

Once I had a bunch of thyme
I thought it never would decay
Then came a lusty sailor, who chanced to pass my way,
And stole my bunch of thyme away.

Come all ye, etc.

The sailor gave to me a rose
A rose that never would decay
He gave it to me to keep me reminded
Of when he stole my thyme away.

Come all ye, etc.

OMB 77

# As I Roved Out

And who are you me pret-ty fair___ maid and who are you me

ho-ney, And who are you me pret-ty fair___maid and who are you me ho-ney, She

ans-wered me quite___ mo-dest-ly; 'I am me moth-ers dar-ling, With me

too-ry-ay, Fol de did-dle day, Di-re, Fol de did-dle dair-ie___ oh, ___

And will you come to me mother's house
When the sun is shining clearly (repeat)
I'll open the door and I'll let you in
And divil a one would hear us.

So I went to her house in the middle of the night
When the moon was shining clearly (repeat)
She opened the door and she let me in
And divil the one did hear us.

She took me horse by the bridle and the bit
And she led him to the stable (repeat)
Saying, 'There's plenty of oats for a soldier's horse,
To eat it if he's able.'

The she took me by the lily-white hand,
And she led me to the table (repeat)
Saying, 'There's plenty of wine for a soldier boy,
To drink it if you're able.'

Then I got up and made the bed
And I made it nice and aisy  (repeat)
Then I got up and laid her down,
Saying, 'Lassie, are you able?'

And there we lay till the break of day,
And divil a one did hear us  (repeat)
Then I arose and put on me clothes,
Saying, 'Lassie, I must leave you.'

And when will you return again
And when will we get married  (repeat)
When broken shells make Christmas bells
We might well get married.

*Carrickfergus Castle—from the land side.*

# Carrickfergus

I wish I was__ in Car - rick - fer - gus,____ on - ly for nights__ in Bal - ly - grant I would swim o - ver the deep - est o - cean,____ on - ly for nights__ in Bal - ly - grant.__ __ But the sea is wide____ and I can't swim o - ver____ nor have__ I the wings to fly____ if I could find me a hand - some boats - man____ to fer - ry me o - ver to my love and die.____

Now in Kilkenny, it is reported,
They've marble stones as black as ink,
With gold and silver I would transport her,
But I'll sing no more now 'till I get a drink.
I'm drunk today, but then I'm seldom sober,
A handsome rover from town to town.
Ah, but I'm sick now, my days are over,
Come all ye young lads and lay me down.

# The Flower of Sweet Strabane

If I were king of Ireland and all things at my will, I'd
roam for re - cre - a - tion, no com - forts to find still, Of
com - forts I would like the best as you might un - der - stand is to
win the heart of Mar - tha the flo - wer of sweet Stra - bane.

Her cheeks they are a rosy red, her hair golden brown
And o'er her lily white shoulders it carelessly falls down
She's one of the loveliest creatures of the whole creation planned
And my heart is captivated by the Flower of Sweet Strabane.

If I had you lovely Martha away in Innishowen
Or in some lonesome valley in the wild woods of Tyrone
I would use my whole endeavour and I'd try to work my plan
For to gain my prize and to feast my eyes on the Flower of Sweet Strabane.

Oh, I'll go o'er the Lagan down by the steam ships tall
I'm sailing for Amerikay across the briny foam
My boat is bound for Liverpool down by the Isle of Man
So I'll say farewell, God bless you, my Flower of Sweet Strabane.

OMB 77

# The Shores of Amerikay

I'm bid - ding fare - well to the land of my youth and the home I love so well,____ And the moun - tains so grand in my own na - tive land I am bid - ding them all fare - well,____ With an ach - in' heart I'll bid them a - dieu, for to - mor - row I'll sail far a - way,____ O'er the ra - ging foam for to seek a home on the shores of A - me - ri - kay.

It's not for the want of employment I'm going,
It's not for the love of fame,
That fortune bright may shine over me,
And give me a glorious name.
It's not for the want of employment I'm going,
O'er the weary and stormy sea,
But to seek a home for my own true love,
On the shores of Amerikay.

And when I'm bidding my last farewell,
The tears like rain will blind,
To think of my friends in my own native land
And the home I'm leaving behind.
But if I'm to die in a foreign land,
And be buried so far away,
No fond mother's tears will be shed o'er my grave
On the shores of Amerikay.

# The Praties

Oh the pra-ties* they grow small o-ver here, o-ver here, Oh the pra-ties they grow small o-ver here. Oh the pra-ties they grow small and we dig them in the fall, and we eat them coats and all, o-ver here, o-ver here.

Oh I wish that we were geese, night and morn, night and morn
Oh I wish that we were geese, night and morn,
Oh I wish that we were geese and could live our lives in peace
Till the hour of our release, eating corn, eating corn.

Oh we're down into the dust over here, over here,
Oh we're down into the dust over here,
Oh we're down into the dust, but the Lord in whom we trust,
Will repay us crumb for crust, over here, over here.

*potatoes

*Carrig-a-Droid Castle.*

OMB 77

# The Curragh of Kildare

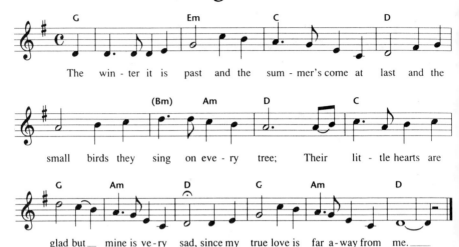

The win-ter it is past and the sum-mer's come at last and the small birds they sing on eve-ry tree; Their lit-tle hearts are glad but— mine is ve-ry sad, since my true love is far a-way from me.——

The rose upon the briar, by the water running clear,
Gives joy to the linnet and the bee;
Their little hearts are blest, but mine is not at rest,
While my true love is absent from me.

A livery I'll wear, and I'll comb back my hair,
And in velvet so green I will appear;
And straight I will repair to the Curragh of Kildare,
For it's there I'll find tidings of my dear.

I'll wear a cap of black, with a frill around my neck,
Gold rings on my fingers I wear;
It's this I undertake, for my true lover's sake,
He resides at the Curragh of Kildare.

I would not think it strange, thus the world for to range,
If I only got tidings of my dear;
But here in Cupid's chain, if I'm bound to remain,
I would spend my whole life in despair.

My love is like the sun, that in the firmament does run;
And always proves constant and true;
But his is like the moon, that wanders up and down,
And every month is new.

All you that are in love and cannot it remove,
I pit the pains you endure;
For experience let me know, that your hearts are full of woe,
And a woe that no mortal can cure.

# My Mary of the Curling Hair

By Gerald Griffin

My Ma-ry of the cur-ling hair, the laugh-ing cheeks and bash-ful air, A

bri-dal morn is dawn-ing fair with blush-es in the skies.

*Chorus*

Siúl,___ siúl,___ siúl a rún siúl go so-cair a-gus siúl go ciúin, My

love, my pearl, my own dear girl, My moun-tain maid___ a - rise.

For we were known from infancy,
Thy father's hearth was home to me,
No selfish love was mine for thee,
Unholy and unwise.

I am no stranger proud and gay,
To win thee from thy home away,
And find thee for a distant day
A theme for wasting sights.

But soon my love shall be my bride,
And happy by our own fireside,
My veins shall feel the rosy tide,
Which lingering hope denies.

OMB 77

# The Wild Colonial Boy

There was a wild co-lo-nial boy, Jack Dug-gan was his name___ ___ He was born and raised in Ire-land in a place called Cast-le-main,_ ___ He was his fath-er's on-ly son, his moth-er's pride and joy,___ ___ And dear-ly did his pa-rents love the Wild Co-lo-nial Boy.___

At the early age of sixteen years he left his native home,
And through Australia's sunny clime he was inclined to roam.
He robbed the lordly squatters, their flocks he would destroy,
A terror to Australia was the Wild Colonial Boy.

For two long years this daring youth ran on his wild career,
With a heart that knew no danger, their justice did not fear.
He stuck the Beechworth coach up, and he robbed Judge McEvoy,
Who, trembling, gave his gold up to the Wild Colonial Boy.

He bade the judge 'Good morning' and he told him to beware,
For he never robbed an honest judge what acted 'on the square'.
'Yet you would rob a mother of her son and only joy,
And breed a race of outlaws like the Wild Colonial Boy.'

One morning on the prairie Wild Jack Duggan rode along,
While listening to the mocking birds singing a cheerful song.
Out jumped three troopers fierce and grim, Kelly, Davis and FitzRoy,
They all set out to capture him, the Wild Colonial Boy.

'Surrender now, Jack Duggan, you can see there's three to one,
Surrender in the Queen's name, sir, you are a plundering son.'
Jack drew two pistols from his side and glared upon FitzRoy,
'I'll fight, but not surrender', cried the Wild Colonial Boy.

He fired point blank at Kelly and brought him to the ground.
He fired a shot at Davis, too who fell dead at the sound,
But a bullet pierced his brave young heart from the pistol of FitzRoy,
And that was how they captured him - the Wild Colonial Boy.

*Shandon Steeple.*

OMB 77

# In Scartaglen There Lived a Lass

In Scar - ta - glen there lived a lass, and ev' - ry Sun - day
af - ter mass, she would go and take a glass, be -
fore goin' home by Bear - na. We won't go home a -
long the road, for fear that you might act the rogue,
Won't go home a - long the road, We'll go home by Bear - na.

We won't go home across the fields
The big thorníns could stick in your heels.
We won't go home across the fields;
We'll go home by Bearna.

We won't go home around the glen
For fear your blood might rise again
Won't go home around the glen
But we'll go home by Bearna.

We won't go down the milk boreen
The night is bright we might be seen
We won't go down the milk boreen
But we'll go home by Bearna.

We won't go home across the bog
In fear we might meet Kearney's dog.
We won't go home across the bog
But we'll go home by Bearna.

# Will You Come to the Bower

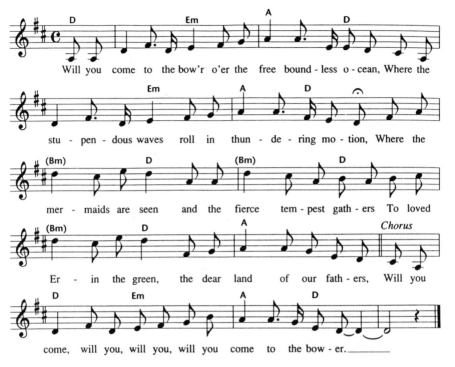

Will you come to the bow'r o'er the free bound-less o-cean, Where the stu-pen-dous waves roll in thun-de-ring mo-tion, Where the mer-maids are seen and the fierce tem-pest gath-ers To loved Er-in the green, the dear land of our fath-ers, Will you come, will you, will you, will you come to the bow-er.

Will you come to the land of O'Neill and O'Donnell,
Of Lord Lucan of old and the immortal O'Connell.
Where Brian drove the Danes and St. Patrick the vermin,
And whose valleys remain still most beautiful and charming

You can visit Benburb and the storied Blackwater,
Where Owen Roe met Munroe and his chieftains did slaughter
Where the lambs skip and play on the mossey all over
From those golden bright views to enchanting Rostrevor.

You can see Dublin city and the fine groves of Blarney,
The Bann, the Boyne, the Liffey and the lakes of Killarney;
You may ride on the tide o'er the broad majestic Shannon,
You may sail round Lough Neagh and see storied Dungannon.

You can visit New Ross, gallant Wexford and Gorey,
Where the green grass was last seen by proud Saxon and Tory,
Where the soil is sanctified by the blood of each true man,
Where they died satisfied, their enemies they would not run from.

Will you come and awake our lost land from its slumber,
And her fetters we will break, links that long are encumbered
And the air will resound with Hosanna to greet you,
On the shore will be found gallant Irishmen to meet you.

OMB 77

**Publisher's Note :**
The majority of songs included in this collection follow the same format of
our well-known *'Folksongs and Ballads Popular in Ireland'* by John Loesberg.
The 'Folksongs and Ballads' series features no less than 200 songs
within the four volumes available.
Information on the origins of each song is also included.

**Folksongs and Ballads Popular in Ireland, Volume 1**
collected, edited and arranged by John Loesberg
(OMB 1)
**Folksongs and Ballads Popular in Ireland, Volume 2**
(OMB 2)
**Folksongs and Ballads Popular in Ireland, Volume 3**
(OMB 3)
**Folksongs and Ballads Popular in Ireland, Volume 4**
(OMB 4)

**Ossian Publications** produce a huge range of Irish Music,
ranging from Sheetmusic, Songbooks, Tune Collections,
Instruction Books to an acclaimed catalogue of
Traditional Irish Music on CD.
For a complete list of all our publications please send your
name and address to:

**•Ossian Publications Ltd.•**
P.O.Box 84, Cork, Ireland
ossian@iol.ie

OSSIAN